A CourseGuide for

A Theology of Luke and Acts

Darrell L. Bock

ZONDERVAN ACADEMIC

A CourseGuide for A Theology of Luke and Acts
Copyright © 2020 by Zondervan

Requests for information should be addressed to:
Zondervan, *3900 Sparks Dr. SE, Grand Rapids, Michigan 49546*

ISBN 978-0-310-11122-1 (softcover)

All Scripture quotations, unless otherwise indicated, are taken from The Holy Bible, New International Version®, NIV®. Copyright © 1973, 1978, 1984, 2011 by Biblica, Inc.® Used by permission of Zondervan. All rights reserved worldwide. www.Zondervan.com. The "NIV" and "New International Version" are trademarks registered in the United States Patent and Trademark Office by Biblica, Inc.®

Any internet addresses (websites, blogs, etc.) and telephone numbers in this book are offered as a resource. They are not intended in any way to be or imply an endorsement by Zondervan, nor does Zondervan vouch for the content of these sites and numbers for the life of this book.

No part of this publication may be reproduced, stored in a retrieval system, or transmitted in any form or by any means — electronic, mechanical, photocopy, recording, or any other — except for brief quotations in printed reviews, without the prior permission of the publisher.

Printed in the United States of America

CONTENTS

Introduction 5

1. and 2. The Often-Lost Importance of Luke-Acts and the Orientation of this Study and The Context of Luke-Acts: A Short Introduction 7

3. The Case for the Unity of Luke-Acts and Reading the Volumes as Luke-Acts and as Luke and Acts. 11

4. Outline and Narrative Survey of Luke-Acts 15

5. The Plan, Activity, and Character of God: A Survey in Narrative Order 19

6. The God of Promise, Fulfillment, and Salvation: Synthesis of Texts on the Plan of God 22

7. Jesus the Messiah Who Is Lord and Bringer of the New Era: Narrative Order 25

8. Messiah, Servant, Prophet, Savior, Son of Man, and Lord: A Synthesis on the Person and Work of Jesus 29

9. The Holy Spirit in Luke-Acts: Power and Enablement for the Promise and Witness of the New Era. 33

10. The Salvation of God through Christ and the Healings That Picture It: Narrative Order. 37

11. The Many Dimensions of Salvation in Luke-Acts: A Synthesis 40

12. Israel in Luke-Acts 43

13. **The Gentiles and the Expression "the Nations" in Luke-Acts** 47

14. **The Church and the Way in Luke-Acts** 51

15. **Discipleship and Ethics in the New Community** 54

16. **How Response to Jesus Divides: The Opponents, the Crowds, and Rome as Observer of Events in Luke-Acts** 58

17. **Women, the Poor, and the Social Dimensions in Luke-Acts** ... 62

18. **The Law in Luke-Acts** 67

19. **Ecclesiology in Luke-Acts** 70

20. **Eschatology, Judgment, and Hope for the Future in Luke-Acts** 74

21. **The Scriptures in Luke-Acts** 78

22. **Luke-Acts in the Canon** 82

23. **Conclusion** 85

Introduction

Welcome to the *A CourseGuide for A Theology of Luke and Acts*. These guides were created for formal and informal students alike who want to engage deeper in biblical, theological, or ministry studies. We hope this guide will provide an opportunity for you to grow not only in your understanding, but also in your faith.

How to Use This Guide

This guide is meant to be used in conjunction with the book *A Theology of Luke and Acts* and its corresponding videos, *A Theology of Luke and Acts, A Video Study*. After you have read each chapter in the book and watched the accompanying video lesson, the materials in this guide will help you review and assess what you have learned. Application-oriented questions are included as well.

Each CourseGuide has been individually designed to best equip you in your studies, but in general, you can expect the following components. Most CourseGuides begin every chapter with a "You Should Know" section, which highlights key terminology, people, and facts to remember. This section serves as a helpful summary for directing your studies. Reflection questions, typically two to three per chapter, prompt you to summarize key points you've learned. Discussion questions invite you to an even deeper level of engagement. Finally, most chapters will end with a short quiz to test your retention. You can find the answer key to each quiz at the bottom of the page following it.

For Further Study

CourseGuides accompany books and videos from some of the world's top biblical and theological scholars. They may be used independently, or in small groups or classrooms, offering quality instruction to equip students for academic and ministry pursuits. If you would like to engage in further study with Zondervan's CourseGuides, the full lineup may be viewed online. After completing your studies with *A CourseGuide for A Theology of Luke and Acts*, we recommend moving on to *A CourseGuide for Four Views on the Apostle Paul* and *A CourseGuide for Introduction to Biblical Interpretation*.

CHAPTERS 1 AND 2

The Often-Lost Importance of Luke–Acts and the Orientation of this Study and The Context of Luke–Acts: A Short Introduction

You Should Know

- Luke wrote the most of any New Testament author, wrote his works from an unknown location, and wrote Luke-Acts in a unified form.

- Luke thought the community of saints were persecuted in Acts because it was according to God's design since they follow Jesus.

- The obstacle Luke was seeking to overcome through his narratives was that the community was worshiping a dead Savior and suffering persecution in a community that included the Gentiles.

- Reasons for suggesting Luke wrote Luke-Acts: the early church believed Luke was the author; the use of "we" in Acts; the relationship of Luke to the other gospels in their sequence

- The eschatological discourses of Jesus is the most central argument for dating Luke-Acts between AD 80–90.

- Mark: the source modern scholarship thinks Luke heavily relied upon

- Ancient *bios*: biographies written during the time of the Greco-Roman era detailing major events in the subject's life

- Historical monograph: a document containing historical prose that is selective in the events it portrays in order to convey a point

Essay Questions

Short

1. Why does the connection between Luke and Acts tend to be neglected by many readers of Scripture? What evidence is there that Luke wrote the gospel traditionally ascribed to him and the book of Acts?

2. When was Luke-Acts most likely written? Why?

3. What is an ancient *bios* and how is it different from modern biographies?

Long

1. Is Luke a faithful historian when he interprets and connects various events in a theological manner? Why or why not? Can history be presented as more than a mere reporting of facts? Why or why not?

Quiz

1. (T/F) Luke wrote the largest portion of the New Testament out of all the New Testament authors.

2. Which of the following obstacles did Luke set out to overcome to provide assurance to Theophilus, Luke's intended audience:
    a) Support from Roman authorities
    b) A dead Savior
    c) A persecuted community that included Gentiles
    d) Both B & C
    e) Both A & C

3. Luke proved that the community of saints suffered because:
    a) They were punished for rejecting Jesus
    b) They were under judgment for straying from the Old Covenant
    c) It was according to God's design to atone for their sins
    d) It was according to God's design since they follow Jesus

4. Which of the following is NOT considered a reason to suggest Luke wrote Luke-Acts?
    a) The early church's belief that Luke was the author
    b) The use of "they" in Acts
    c) The open ending of Acts
    d) The relationship of Luke to the other gospels in their sequence

5. (T/F) Church tradition is unified in all the facts concerning Luke's life and history.

6. (T/F) Per Bock, Luke's gospel was ascribed to Luke to establish credibility for the author who wrote it.

7. The most central argument for dating Luke-Acts between AD 80–90 is:
    a) Paul's emergence as a hero
    b) The eschatological discourses of Jesus
    c) The "early catholic" theology
    d) Pre-Domitian persecution

8. In contemporary scholarship, the common view of the source Luke relied heavily upon is:
    a) Matthew
    b) Mark
    c) Q
    d) Clement

9. Which is NOT an argument for dating Luke-Acts in the AD 60s?
    a) Jesus's predictions of the eschatological end
    b) The silence about Jerusalem's destruction
    c) Failure to note the death of James or Paul
    d) Uncertainty regarding Gentile-Jewish relations

10. Luke wrote his gospel in:
    a) Rome
    b) Antioch
    c) An unknown location
    d) Caesarea

ANSWER KEY

1. T, 2. D, 3. D, 4. B, 5. F, 6. F, 7. B, 8. B, 9. A, 10. C

CHAPTER 3

The Case for the Unity of Luke–Acts and Reading the Volumes as Luke–Acts and as Luke and Acts

You Should Know

- The idea that Luke-Acts was one work was lost in the logical division of the canon along the lines of gospel and early church history. It was recovered in the early twentieth century when NT scholars began to speak of Luke-Acts, using a hyphen to tie together these two NT books.

- What is intended in saying that Luke-Acts is a unity is the idea that Luke wrote his gospel with the goal of writing Acts later in order to tell one basic story.

- The idea that Luke-Acts should be read as a single unit gained great momentum from the work of H. J. Cadbury, especially his volume *The Making of Luke-Acts*.

- Mikeal Parsons and Richard Pervo challenge the unity view by looking at the issues of genre, narrative, and theology, questioning how much unity can be brought to the account, preferring to see "independent but interrelated works."

- The range of narrative connections and links between Luke and Acts suggests that Luke used his sources and, however diverse they were, he sought to weave them into a singular account and a core story line.

- We read Luke-Acts as Luke-Acts on the basis of its literary and theological unity, not on the basis of its being issued as two volumes from one author.

- Theophilus: the man who commissioned Luke to write the historical narrative of Luke-Acts

Essay Questions

Short

1. What is intended in saying that Luke-Acts is a unity?

2. Explain how the idea of reading Luke-Acts as a unity is challenged.

Long

1. Explain and summarize the reasons why we read Luke-Acts as a single Luke-Acts.

Quiz

1. (T/F) According to Bock, Luke-Acts is a unified narrative.

2. Speaking of Luke-Acts as a unity is the idea that:
    a) Luke wrote his gospel and only later thought about writing Acts to continue the story.
    b) Luke wrote his gospel with the goal of writing Acts later in order to tell one basic story.
    c) Luke wrote one book and split it into two volumes.
    d) Luke wrote two books and joined them into one.

3. The idea that Luke-Acts should be read as a single unit gained great momentum from the work of
   a) H. J. Cadbury
   b) Richard Pervo
   c) Mikeal Parsons
   d) N.T. Wright

4. (T/F) The limited number of narrative connections and links suggests that Luke used his sources and used this diversity to write two separate accounts.

5. Bock suggests we read Luke-Acts as Luke-Acts on the basis of:
   a) Its literary unity
   b) Its theological unity
   c) Its being issued as two volumes from one author
   d) A & B
   e) A & C

6. The wrestling in Acts with exactly how to include _____ showed one of the first key issues the church had to resolve.
   a) Jews
   b) Romans
   c) Gentiles
   d) Greeks

7. Who in Luke-Acts molded the way of life the unifying storyline outlines regarding life in the new age?
   a) Jesus
   b) Peter
   c) Paul
   d) All of the above

8. Who was it who could be reassured through Luke-Acts that as a Gentile he was part of a movement that started out Jewish and was facing pressure all around?
   a) Luke
   b) Theophilus

c) Paul
d) Timothy

9. Which of the following texts suggests to reading Luke and Acts together?

a) Luke 1:1–4
b) Luke 14:15–24
c) Luke 21:12–19
d) All of the above

10. (T/F) C. Kavin Rowe suggests we should read Luke-Acts as a unit and as Luke and Acts in order to avoid making too much of a topical break or of losing the connections between the books.

ANSWER KEY

1. T, 2. B, 3. A, 4. F, 5. D, 6. C, 7. D, 8. B, 9. D, 10. T

CHAPTER 4

Outline and Narrative Survey of Luke–Acts

You Should Know

- Luke 1:1–4: "Inasmuch as many have undertaken to compile a narrative of the things that have been accomplished among us, just as those who from the beginning were eyewitnesses and ministers of the word have delivered them to us, it seemed good to me also, having followed all things closely for some time past, to write an orderly account for you, most excellent Theophilus, that you may have certainty concerning the things you have been taught."

- Things begin to turn in Luke's gospel at Peter's confession of Jesus as the Christ.

- The primary reason that Jesus was finally condemned by the Jewish religious leaders and sent to Pilate was his declaration to the religious leaders that he is the Christ.

- AD 70 is the date of the destruction of Jerusalem predicted by Jesus.

- The coming of the Spirit is made evident through speaking in tongues, as all believers are clothed with the Spirit as Joel 2:28–32 promised about "the last days."

- The new community of Christ gathered around the apostolic teaching, fellowship, the breaking of bread, and prayer. They also voluntarily shared all things in common, showing their love and commitment to each other.

- The outreach to Gentiles becomes established in Acts 15 at the Jerusalem Council and the church continues to be strengthened.

- Through Luke-Acts Theophilus can know that he belongs in God's movement in Christ that had Jewish roots but is intended for all by divine promise and direction.

- Mary: mother of Jesus; Luke wrote his infancy narrative from her perspective

- Christ: Greek word for "Messiah" or "anointed one"

Essay Questions

Short

1. Why do things begin to turn in Luke's gospel at Peter's confession of Jesus as the Christ?

2. Why was the primary reason that Jesus was finally condemned by the Jewish religious leaders and sent to Pilate due to his declaration to the religious leaders that he is the Christ?

3. Explain the events of Cornelius and how they later connected to the consultation and council at Jerusalem.

Long

1. Create your own outline of the book of Luke using Bock's as your example. Create your own outline of the book of Acts using Bock's as your example.

Quiz

1. According to Bock, the infancy narrative of Luke is told primarily from the perspective of:
    a) Mary
    b) Joseph
    c) Elizabeth
    d) Jesus

2. According to Bock, things begin to turn in Luke's gospel at:

   a) John's declaration that Jesus is the Son of God
   b) Peter's confession of Jesus as the Christ
   c) Jesus's crucifixion on the cross
   d) The birth of Jesus

3. The destruction of Jerusalem that Jesus predicted occurred in:

   a) AD 70
   b) AD 60
   c) AD 80
   d) AD 90

4. Jesus was finally condemned by the religious leaders and sent to Pilate for saying:

   a) He would destroy the temple.
   b) He was the second Moses.
   c) He was the Christ.
   d) He would overthrow the religious leaders.

5. In what way was the coming of the Spirit made evident at the outset of the early church?

   a) Through sermons
   b) Through social justice
   c) Through evangelism
   d) Through speaking in tongues

6. What triggered the bulk of the early church community to be forced out of Jerusalem into Judea and Samaria?

   a) The death of Jesus
   b) The martyrdom of Stephen
   c) The Council of Jerusalem
   d) The trial of Paul

7. Jesus had chosen Saul to take the gospel before:

   a) Gentiles
   b) Kings
   c) The Jews
   d) All of the above

8. What key section of Acts treats the expansion of the gospel to the Gentiles, which God directs and is responsible for initiating?
   a) Acts 2:1–41
   b) Acts 9:32–12:25
   c) Acts 10:1–11:18
   d) Acts 13:1–14:28

9. (T/F) Through Luke-Acts Theophilus can know that he belongs in this movement of God that had Jewish roots and was only intended for him by divine promise and direction.

10. (T/F) Luke-Acts is ultimately a book about God and his activity through Jesus, in whose name much in Acts takes place.

ANSWER KEY

1. A, 2. B, 3. A, 4. C, 5. D, 6. B, 7. D, 8. C, 9. F, 10. T

CHAPTER 5

The Plan, Activity, and Character of God: A Survey in Narrative Order

You Should Know

- Adam was the first man created by God, brought the fall by his disobedience, and is called the "son of God" in Luke's genealogy.

- Certain narrative techniques Scripture used in biblical narrative include: the use of Scripture to comment on and reveal God's purposes; the comments of reliable characters within the narrative; and the emergence of God's purpose through commissioned agents

- Abraham: father of the Jews and the one to whom God revealed his promises to Israel that would later bless the Gentiles as well

- John the Baptist warned that descent from Abraham does not automatically qualify one for salvation by saying that God can raise children of Abraham from stones.

- Jesus taught his disciples before he ascended about the timing of his return that it was not their concern.

- Soteriology: the doctrine of how God saves man

- Already: designation for eschatological or end time realities that are already present in this age

- Not yet: designation for eschatological or end time realities that will come in the future age

Essay Questions

Short

1. What do the hymns in the infancy narrative of Jesus tell us about God's character and work?

2. What does John the Baptist's ministry tell us about God's character and work?

3. How does Luke teach us about the work of Christ by ascribing to Christ work that should be ascribed to God?

Long

1. What does the book of Acts tell us about God's character and work? Cite specific examples, tracing this work from beginning to end.

Quiz

1. The doctrine of salvation is called:
    a) Eschatology
    b) Hamartiology
    c) Anthropology
    d) Soteriology

2. (T/F) Adam was the first man created by God, brought the fall by his disobedience, and is called the "son of God" in Luke's genealogy.

3. (T/F) The dominant actor in Luke-Acts is God.

4. According to Bock, all of the following are narrative techniques Scripture uses in biblical narrative except for:
    a) The emergence of God's purpose through commissioned agents
    b) The comments of reliable characters within the narrative
    c) The appeal to the personal inspiration of the reader
    d) The use of Scripture to comment on and reveal God's purposes

5. The keystone for understanding the center of Luke's soteriology is:
    a) Love
    b) Humility

c) Jesus
d) Grace

6. John the Baptist warned that descent from Abraham does not automatically qualify one for salvation because:
   a) God is able to raise children of Abraham from stones.
   b) God favors descendants of Abraham who follow the law of Moses.
   c) John is a Gentile.
   d) God saves only those descended from Jacob.

7. (T/F) Jesus was the only person that Luke called the son of God.

8. The kingdom of God is:
   a) Already
   b) Not yet
   c) Neither A nor B
   d) Both A & B

9. Per Bock, Jesus taught believers in Acts that the timing of his return:
   a) Would be known to them shortly before he returns
   b) Was not their concern
   c) Could be predicted through reading Scripture
   d) Would be known only to the apostles

10. The final reference to God in Acts takes place as Paul announces that the salvation of God has been sent to whom, affirming the mission to this group of people that Luke-Acts has sought in part to affirm and defend?
    a) Jews
    b) Romans
    c) Gentiles
    d) Greeks

ANSWER KEY
1. D, 2. T, 3. T, 4. C, 5. C, 6. A, 7. F, 8. D, 9. B, 10. C

CHAPTER 6

The God of Promise, Fulfillment, and Salvation: Synthesis of Texts on the Plan of God

You Should Know

- God's act of mercy in sending Jesus Christ was rooted in his promises to Abraham.

- Agents of revelation include: direct revelation, human agents, and angelic agents

- Without neglecting the importance of the other aspects, the most crucial element of Jesus's work according to Luke is his exaltation.

- When he told his disciples to go and make the message of forgiveness known to all nations, he meant Jews as well as Gentiles.

- The distribution of the Holy Spirit at Pentecost proved that Jesus Christ is now at the right hand of his Father.

- Jesus's mission in Luke: calling sinners to repentance

- Ends of the earth: a reference that includes all peoples and locales whether Jew or Gentile

- Inaugurated eschatology: an eschatology in which the promises of God are already present, but not yet fully realized in their fullness

Essay Questions

Short

1. Does Luke teach that salvation of the Gentiles stems back to God's original plan in the Hebrew Scriptures? Defend your answer.

2. What does Luke teach about the kingdom of God in Luke-Acts?

3. According to Luke, how did the Holy Spirit guide the believing community in Acts? How does the Spirit still guide the church today?

Long

1. What Lucan theme illustrating the picture of God's divine plan do you resonate most with? Why? Which theme do you see most clearly in today's church?

Quiz

1. God's act of mercy in sending Jesus Christ was rooted in:
    a) God's promises to Abraham
    b) John the Baptist's promises to Israel
    c) The Gentiles' desire for salvation
    d) Israel's unfaithfulness

2. How does God direct his plan? He administers it through various means, including:
    a) Revelation
    b) Divine intervention including portents, dreams, and rescues
    c) The work of agents, both human and angelic
    d) The work of Christ himself
    e) All of the above

3. In revealing himself and his work of salvation, God uses:
    a) Direct revelation
    b) Human agents
    c) Angelic agents
    d) All of the above

4. According to Bock, without neglecting the importance of the other aspects, for Luke the most crucial element of Jesus's work was: (p. 130)
   a) Crucifixion
   b) Exaltation
   c) Birth
   d) Earthly ministry

5. When Jesus told his disciples to go and make the message of forgiveness known to all nations, he meant: (p. 133)
   a) Jews as well as Gentiles
   b) Hellenistic Jews
   c) Jews scattered in the exile
   d) Anyone who was circumcised

6. According to Bock, Jesus defined his divine calling and mission as: (p. 136–137)
   a) Calling sinners to repentance
   b) Teaching a new ethic
   c) Enduring Satan's temptations
   d) Restoring reason to men's minds

7. According to Bock, "ends of the earth" refers to: (p. 138)
   a) Rome
   b) All people and locales
   c) Gentiles
   d) Undiscovered lands

8. Per Bock, Luke viewed the kingdom of God as: (pg. 142)
   a) Politically visible
   b) Fully arrived
   c) Fading
   d) Inaugurated

9. (T/F) The distribution of the Holy Spirit at Pentecost proved that Jesus Christ is now at the right hand of his Father.

10. (T/F) The way to God was the way sought by the Jewish leaders.

ANSWER KEY

1. A, 2. E, 3. D, 4. B, 5. A, 6. A, 7. B, 8. D, 9. T, 10. F

CHAPTER 7

Jesus the Messiah Who Is Lord and Bringer of the New Era: Narrative Order

You Should Know

- When Luke used the title "Son of God" for Jesus Christ, his purpose for using that title was to describe Jesus's office.

- When Simeon predicted the rising and falling of many in Israel at Jesus's coming, he was referring to two groups of people: one accepted Jesus in faith and the other rejected Jesus.

- Luke 1:49: "And [Jesus] said to them, 'Why were you looking for me? Did you not know that I must be in my Father's house?'"

- Jesus's healing of a paralytic early in Luke's narrative proved about Jesus that he was also able to forgive sins.

- In Luke's account of the transfiguration, when God says "listen to him," this was alluding to the prophet Moses predicted would come.

- Deuteronomy 18:15: "The Lord your God will raise up for you a prophet like me from among you, from your brothers–it is to him you shall listen."

- Jerusalem Council: council in Acts 15 where the church recognized the full inclusion of the Gentiles without their having to become Jews

- The designation of Jesus as "Lord" shows an overlap with the God of Israel in terms of functions like forgiveness, the distribution of the Spirit, the offer of salvation in his name, and the coming exercise of judgment.

Essay Questions

Short

1. Pick three titles or attributes given to Jesus in his infancy narrative and explain what they teach the reader about Christ. (p. 150–159)

2. According to Bock, what did Jesus mean when he called himself the "Son of Man"?

3. How does the book of Acts prove that Jesus is alone the Lord of salvation?

Long

1. If someone told you that Luke did not believe Jesus Christ was God, how would you respond?

Quiz

1. (T/F) According to Bock, Luke's Christology is haphazard and lacks coherence.

2. Per Bock, when Luke used the title "Son of God" for Jesus Christ, his emphasis was one of:
    a) Ontology
    b) Jewish descent
    c) Office
    d) None of the above

3. According to Bock, when Simeon predicted the rising and falling of many in Israel at Jesus's coming, he was referring to: (p. 157–158)
    a) Two groups of people, one accepted Jesus in faith and the other rejected Jesus

b) One group of people who began in humiliation and ended in exaltation
  c) One group of people who began in exaltation and ended in humiliation
  d) Two groups of people, one Gentile and the other Jewish

4. Bock believes that Jesus's comment to his mother in the temple, after they found him, should be translated: (p. 159)
   a) I must be about my Father's business.
   b) I must be in the things of my Father.
   c) I had to be in my Father's house.
   d) I must be doing my Father's will.

5. (T/F) The Holy Spirit first comes upon Jesus at his baptism.

6. Jesus's healing of a paralytic early in Luke's narrative proves that Jesus:
   a) Was like an Old Testament prophet
   b) Was a great physician
   c) Was able to forgive sins
   d) Was an ally of the Sadducees

7. In Luke's account of the transfiguration, when God says "listen to him," this is an allusion to:
   a) The prophet Moses predicted would come
   b) The king David knew would come from him
   c) The priest Melchizedek promised to Abraham
   d) The son Abraham was promised would come from him

8. (T/F) In Acts, explicit references to the Hebrew Scriptures start to become rare after the gospel message is extended to the Gentiles.

9. Which church council was where the church recognized the full inclusion of the Gentiles without their having to become Jews?
   a) Council of Jamnia
   b) Council of Jerusalem
   c) Council of Nicea
   d) Council of Ephesus

10. The designation of Jesus as "Lord" shows an overlap with the God of Israel in terms of:
   a) Functions like forgiveness
   b) The distribution of the Spirit
   c) The offer of salvation in his name
   d) The coming exercise of judgment
   e) All of the above

ANSWER KEY

1. F, 2. C, 3. A, 4. C, 5. F, 6. C, 7. A, 8. T, 9. B, 10. E

CHAPTER 8

Messiah, Servant, Prophet, Savior, Son of Man, and Lord: A Synthesis on the Person and Work of Jesus

You Should Know

- The first hint in Luke's gospel that there will be suffering in Jesus's ministry is the promise that Mary will experience pain.
- Psalm 110:1: "The Lord says to my Lord: 'Sit at my right hand, until I make your enemies your footstool.'"
- Jesus didn't use the title "Christ" until the end of his ministry because he wanted the title to be used according to his own terms and understanding.
- Son of Man: title used often by Jesus for himself; alludes to Daniel's vision of the Son of Man in Daniel 7
- The Suffering Servant: Jesus's status as servant during his earthly ministry when he suffered and died on behalf of his people
- The Glorified Servant: Jesus's status as servant during his heavenly reign after his resurrection and ascension when he rules over his church until he comes again a second time
- Resurrection: the bodily resurrection of Christ after he lay buried for three days after his crucifixion

- Ascension: the bodily ascent of Jesus to heaven to sit at the Father's right hand where he rules in glory

Essay Questions

Short

1. What was Luke emphasizing when he used the title of Savior, albeit rarely?

2. How did Luke explain the meaning of the title "Christ"? How does a suffering Christ affect the church's perspective on her ministry?

3. How did Luke parallel the ministry of Elijah and Elisha to Jesus's prophetic role?

Long

1. How did Luke depict the reign of Jesus over his kingdom prior to his second coming? What ways do you think the church can daily live in light of this understanding?

Quiz

1. What covenant was the core promise that led to a messianic hope later in Jewish expectation?
    a) Mosaic
    b) Abrahamic
    c) Davidic
    d) Noahic

2. According to Bock, in Luke's gospel the first allusion to Jesus's coming suffering was:
    a) Herod's attempt to kill Jesus
    b) John the Baptist leaping in his mother's womb
    c) Jesus's birth in a manger
    d) The promise that Mary will experience pain

3. Jesus's use of the title "Son of Man" primarily refers to:
   a) God's primary title for the prophet Ezekiel
   b) Cain and Abel's births in Genesis 4
   c) Daniel's vision of the son of man in Daniel 7
   d) Isaiah's vision of the man of sorrows in Isaiah 53

4. (T/F) According to Bock, Jesus's use of David's words in Psalm 110 implied that "Lord" is a more comprehensive and better title for the Messiah than "Son of David."

5. Jesus did not use the title "Christ" until the end of his ministry because:
   a) He wanted the title to be used per his own terms and understanding
   b) He only realized later in his ministry that he was the Christ
   c) He would receive the title after ascending into heaven
   d) He did not want to offend his contemporaries

6. Luke presented Jesus as a "servant" with which emphasis in the gospel of Luke?
   a) The Exiled Servant
   b) The Jewish Servant
   c) The Glorified Servant
   d) The Suffering Servant

7. Luke presented Jesus as a "servant" with which emphasis in the book of Acts?
   a) The Exiled Servant
   b) The Jewish Servant
   c) The Glorified Servant
   d) The Suffering Servant

8. (T/F) Jesus is the savior of mankind without a resurrection and ascension.

9. (T/F) Jesus is bound inseparably to God's program as Messiah-Servant-Prophet-Son of Man-Savior, and above all as Lord.

10. Per Bock, Luke taught that Christ's kingdom:
   a) Is far away
   b) Is near
   c) Has come
   d) Has always been

ANSWER KEY

1. C, 2. D, 3. C, 4. T, 5. A, 6. D, 7. C, 8. F, 9. T, 10. C

CHAPTER 9

The Holy Spirit in Luke–Acts: Power and Enablement for the Promise and Witness of the New Era

You Should Know

- When John the Baptist said the Messiah will baptize with the Spirit and fire, he meant the Messiah gives one baptism of both salvation and judgment.

- Luke's key to seeing the new era has come is the universal distribution or outpouring of the Holy Spirit.

- Joel 2:28–29: "And it shall come to pass afterward, that I will pour out my Spirit on all flesh; your sons and your daughters shall prophesy, your old men shall dream dreams, and your young men shall see visions. Even on the male and female servants in those days I will pour out my Spirit."

- Ananias's lie to the community was ultimately revealed to be a lie towards the Holy Spirit.

- Luke portrays the Spirit as a Spirit of prophecy, salvation, and encouragement.

- Acts: 1:8: "But you will receive power when the Holy Spirit has come upon you, and you will be my witnesses in Jerusalem and in all Judea and Samaria, and to the end of the earth."

- Prophet: an individual filled with the Spirit of God and given direct revelation from God to convey God's will to others

- Adoptionism: a heretical view that Jesus was a man adopted to be the Messiah of God at some point

- Temptation of Jesus: Jesus was led to the temptation by the Holy Spirit; Satan directly confronted and tempted Jesus; unlike Adam, Jesus overcame his temptation.

- Agabus: prophet who predicted a famine and the persecution of Paul in Jerusalem

Essay Questions

Short

1. What was new about the Spirit's coming after Jesus in comparison with the Spirit's presence before Jesus? How is this significant for the church now?

2. How did the Spirit lead the early church in the book of Acts? What do you think Scripture's teaching is concerning the Spirit's leadership now? (p. 220–224)

3. In Acts 21:10–14, does the Spirit's warning through the prophet Agabus as to the consequences of going to Jerusalem contradict the people's statement "Let the will of the Lord be done" in response to Paul's decision to go to Jerusalem anyway? Why or why not? (p. 224)

Long

1. Did Jesus have authority on his own or did it come from the Spirit? Explain your answer.

Quiz

1. (T/F) Luke's depiction of John the Baptist as a prophet is unique because the Holy Spirit fills him for his prophetic role.

2. According to Bock, the baptism of the Spirit and fire is:

    a) Two distinct baptisms of salvation (Spirit) and judgment (fire)
    b) One dividing baptism of both salvation and judgment
    c) Referencing the outpouring of the Spirit at Pentecost
    d) Only destructive judgment

3. A key to seeing that the new era has come is:

    a) The filling of the Spirit in the prophet John the Baptist
    b) The great conversion of all of Israel to the Son of David
    c) The universal distribution or outpouring of the Holy Spirit
    d) The fiery judgment of the Spirit upon the Gentiles

4. After his baptism, Jesus was led into the wilderness by:

    a) Satan
    b) Peter
    c) John the Baptist
    d) The Holy Spirit

5. The coming of the Spirit was a sign of:

    a) The beginning of the first days
    b) The beginning of the last days
    c) The beginning of the second coming
    d) The beginning of faith in God

6. Peter appealed to the promise given in _____ for explaining the significance of the Spirit's outpouring.

    a) Exodus 20
    b) Jeremiah 31
    c) Joel 2
    d) Ezekiel 36

7. Ananias's lie to the community was ultimately lying to:

    a) Peter
    b) The Holy Spirit
    c) James
    d) The church

8. Bock refers to the _____ as the "Pentecost of the Gentile World."

   a) Conversion of Cornelius's household
   b) Reception of the Spirit by the Samaritans
   c) Death of Herod
   d) Conversion of Saul

9. Luke portrayed the Spirit as the Spirit of:

   a) Prophecy
   b) Salvation
   c) Encouragement
   d) All of the above

10. The prophet who warns Paul against going to Jerusalem is:

    a) Agabus
    b) Philip
    c) Simon
    d) Apollos

ANSWER KEY

1. F, 2. B, 3. C, 4. D, 5. B, 6. C, 7. B, 8. A, 9. D, 10. A

CHAPTER 10

The Salvation of God through Christ and the Healings That Picture It: Narrative Order

You Should Know

- σῴζω: Greek word most used by Luke for "save" or "deliver from calamity" (distractors: σωτήρ, σωτηρία, σωτήριος)

- Salvation in Luke's gospel is about responding in faith and trust to what God offers everywhere to people through Jesus.

- Luke 1:51–52 or Mary's Magnificat: He has shown strength with his arm; he has scattered the proud in the thoughts of their hearts; he has brought down the mighty from their thrones and exalted those of humble estate.

- John the Baptist argued that descent from Abraham was not enough to place one in a right relationship with God. He found repentance necessary for one to be in a right relationship.

- Bock defines baptism as a representation of the cleansing that belongs to salvation.

- According to Paul, believing in the Lord Jesus is necessary to be saved.

- At the moment of his resurrection God vindicated Jesus.

- Salvation in Luke is a broad concept. It is about comprehensive deliverance and restoration.

Essay Questions

Short

1. What do the infancy narratives of Jesus in Luke teach about God's coming salvation? How do suffering and glory interplay with one another in our Christian life?

2. From John the Baptist's perspective, what did true repentance look like? What are practical ways believers can respond to God's call to live fruitful lives in keeping with repentance?

3. What does the earthly ministry of Jesus in Luke teach about God's salvation? How does God's full forgiveness of our debts influence our daily lives?

Long

1. How do healings in Luke and Acts illustrate deliverance? Use examples to explain and describe this connection.

Quiz

1. Of the words Luke used to describe God's salvation, _____ is the most commonly used.
    a) σῴζω
    b) σωτήρ
    c) σωτηρία
    d) σωτήριος

2. (T/F) Salvation in Luke's gospel is about responding in faith and trust to what God offers everywhere to people through Jesus.

3. (T/F) Mary's song shows she is aware that the Messiah's suffering precedes glory and is required for vindication from God.

4. For John the Baptist, being descended from Abraham was not enough to be in a relationship with God, but _____ was also necessary.

a) Descent from David
b) Repentance
c) Justice
d) Mercy

5. God vindicated his Son Jesus at his:
   a) Birth
   b) Baptism
   c) Trial
   d) Resurrection

6. According to Bock, baptism is a/an:
   a) Magical act that cleanses one for salvation
   b) Repeatable work that reminds Christians of their place in Christ
   c) Representation of the cleansing that belongs to salvation
   d) Optional act that is useful but not necessary for a believer to do

7. For Paul, what was necessary to be saved?
   a) Believing in the Lord Jesus
   b) Being baptized in the name of God
   c) Performing good works
   d) Refraining from evil works

8. (T/F) Baptism is a representation of the cleansing that belongs to salvation.

9. (T/F) Salvation in Luke is a narrow concept that is about salvation from hell.

10. (T/F) One calls out for God's salvation by calling out in the name of Jesus Christ, the Lord.

ANSWER KEY

1. A, 2. T, 3. F, 4. B, 5. D, 6. C, 7. A, 8. T, 9. F, 10. T

CHAPTER 11

The Many Dimensions of Salvation in Luke–Acts: A Synthesis

You Should Know

- The parable of the prodigal son is a parable in which Luke shows God's initiative to recapture the lost.
- The book of Acts portrays life as a result of the resurrection.
- One's relationship to the final judgment is determined in this life.
- Per Bock, the law is concerned with how others are treated.
- The faith of the centurion that Jesus encounters was unique compared to what Jesus had previously seen because he recognized Jesus's authority, recognized his own unworthiness, and recognized that the power of God is not limited.
- *Shalom*: the Old Testament word for "peace" (distractors: *Shoov*, *Ber'ith*, *Hessed*)
- Preaching: For Luke, this is sharing the salvation message.
- Teaching: For Luke, this includes more than the offer of the gospel.
- Repentance: a reorientation, a total shift of perspective from where one was before repenting

Essay Questions

Short

1. Briefly describe what Luke describes the gospel to be.

2. How did Jesus authenticate his message? What did his miracles and signs teach about his message?

3. Describe the different ways Luke used the word "save" and its variants to teach his readers about salvation. How can knowledge of these different uses help in proclaiming the gospel?

Long

1. Briefly describe and explain each of the benefits of salvation and how you could use each to counsel a believer.

Quiz

1. The gospel notion of "peace" comes from the Old Testament concept of:
   a) *Shoov*
   b) *Ber'ith*
   c) *Shalom*
   d) *Hesed*

2. (T/F) Preaching in Luke-Acts is a broad term encompassing much more than the offer of the gospel, whereas teaching in Luke-Acts tends to be limited to the salvation message.

3. The faith of the centurion that Jesus encountered was unique compared to what Jesus had previously seen because:
   a) The centurion recognized Jesus's authority.
   b) The centurion recognized his own unworthiness.
   c) The centurion recognized that the power of God is not limited.
   d) All of the above

4. Luke showed God's initiative to recapture the lost through:
   a) The parable of the sparrows
   b) The parable of the fountains of living water
   c) The parable of the prodigal son
   d) All of the above

5. The meaning of the word σῴζω is:
   a) To save an animal from a well
   b) To rejoice
   c) To turn from sin
   d) To deliver from calamity

6. (T/F) One's relationship to the final judgment is determined in between this life and the next.

7. (T/F) Repentance is a reorientation, a total shift of perspective from where one was before repenting.

8. In the book of Acts, life is viewed as a result of:
   a) The church
   b) Resurrection
   c) Peace
   d) Perseverance

9. In Luke and Acts, God's promise is portrayed as already-not yet with a judgment tied to:
   a) Jesus's death
   b) The next life
   c) What remains
   d) Sin

10. According to Bock, the law is concerned with:
    a) How others are treated
    b) Giving life
    c) Condemning the righteous
    d) Arbitrary circumstances

ANSWER KEY

1. C, 2. F, 3. D, 4. C, 5. D, 6. F, 7. T, 8. B, 9. C, 10. A

CHAPTER 12

Israel in Luke–Acts

You Should Know

- In Luke's narrative, the entire story of Jesus can be summarized as Israel's story.

- Genesis 12:1–3: "Now the LORD said to Abram, 'Go from your country and your kindred and your father's house to the land that I will show you. And I will make of you a great nation, and I will bless you and make your name great, so that you will be a blessing. I will bless those who bless you, and him who dishonors you I will curse, and in you all the families of the earth shall be blessed.'"

- Jesus suggested that God showed his displeasure to Israel's spiritual condition during the time of Elijah and Elisha by blessing Gentiles.

- Jesus noted the faith of the centurion who asked for the healing of his servant by marveling at his great faith.

- In Jesus's eyes, Israel will no longer receive judgment from God when Israel acknowledges Jesus.

- Luke 22:28–30: "You are those who have stayed with me in my trials, and I assign to you, as my Father assigned to me, a kingdom, that you may eat and drink at my table in my kingdom and sit on thrones judging the twelve tribes of Israel."

- The risen Jesus responded to Peter's question concerning the restoration of Israel by redirecting this concern to focus on his mission.

- Peter described Jesus's preaching during his earthly ministry as the good news of peace.

- Acts 13:22b–24: "He raised up David to be their king, of whom he testified and said, 'I have found in David the son of Jesse a man after my heart, who will do all my will.' Of this man's offspring God has brought to Israel a Savior, Jesus, as he promised. Before his coming, John had proclaimed a baptism of repentance to all the people of Israel."

- Acts 12:6–7: "Now when Herod was about to bring him out, on that very night, Peter was sleeping between two soldiers, bound with two chains, and sentries before the door were guarding the prison. And behold, an angel of the Lord stood next to him, and a light shone in the cell. He struck Peter on the side and woke him, saying, 'Get up quickly.' And the chains fell off his hands."

Essay Questions

Short

1. What do the infancy narratives in Luke teach about Israel and her connection to Christ?

2. What was unexpected about the fulfillment of Psalm 2's promise of persecution towards God's Messiah?

3. How did Paul describe the history of Israel in Acts 13? Why do you think he tells their history in this way?

Long

1. How is the church a continuation of the promises given to Israel of old? Does the church today need to reach out and proclaim the gospel to Jews? Why or why not?

Quiz

1. For Luke, the entire story of Jesus is:
    a) Adam's story
    b) Luke's story
    c) God's story
    d) Israel's story

2. God's promise to bless the nations through Israel was first given to:
    a) Abraham
    b) Mary
    c) John the Baptist
    d) Jacob

3. During the time of Elijah and Elisha, God showed his displeasure with Israel's spiritual condition by: (p. 283)
    a) Blessing Gentiles
    b) Exiling the nation of Israel
    c) Exiling the nation of Judah
    d) Blessing Israel

4. Jesus said that Israel is judged until:
    a) Rome destroys Israel
    b) Jesus is crucified
    c) Israel obeys the law
    d) Israel acknowledges Jesus

5. The disheartened disciples on the road to Emmaus thought that Jesus was the one who would:
    a) Judge Israel
    b) Redeem Israel
    c) Judge the Gentiles
    d) Redeem the Gentiles

6. In response to the disciples' question regarding the restoration of Israel in Acts 1:6, the risen Jesus:
    a) Rebuked this concern
    b) Redirected this concern
    c) Ignored this question
    d) Asked a question in response

7. Peter described Jesus's earthly ministry as a preaching of:
    a) The good news of peace
    b) The good news of Israel
    c) The triumph of the church
    d) The coming of the Gentiles

8. Paul, in describing Israel's history while in Pisidian Antioch with Barnabas, skipped the time between _____ and John the Baptist.

   a) David
   b) Solomon
   c) The restoration
   d) The exodus

9. Peter was saved by _____ when he was imprisoned by Herod.

   a) An earthquake
   b) An apostle
   c) A jailer
   d) An angel

10. When Paul was being persecuted in Jerusalem, the ones who intervened were:

    a) The Romans
    b) The Jews
    c) The apostles
    d) The Pharisees

ANSWER KEY

1. D, 2. A, 3. A, 4. D, 5. B, 6. B, 7. A, 8. A, 9. D, 10. A

CHAPTER 13

The Gentiles and the Expression "the Nations" in Luke–Acts

You Should Know

- Adam is the last person listed in Luke's genealogy of Jesus.

- In contrast to how earthly rulers use their power, Jesus's disciples are called to use their power by being characterized by a spirit of service.

- Luke's gospel *generally* portrays Gentiles as pursuers of wealth and power with no attention for God.

- Amos 9:11–12: "'In that day I will raise up the booth of David that is fallen and repair its breaches, and raise up its ruins and rebuild it as in the days of old, that they may possess the remnant of Edom and all the nations who are called by my name,' declares the LORD who does this."

- Acts 15:27–29: "We have therefore sent Judas and Silas, who themselves will tell you the same things by word of mouth. For it has seemed good to the Holy Spirit and to us to lay on you no greater burden than these requirements: that you abstain from what has been sacrificed to idols, and from blood, and from what has been strangled, and from sexual immorality. If you keep yourselves from these, you will do well. Farewell."

- After Jesus ascended, he continued his task of being a light to the nations through his commissioned servants such as the apostles.

- Luke showed in Acts that God was calling the nations away from their idolatry.
- The Jew and Gentile at times reacted with hostility to the gospel because it was a threat to the way they had lived.
- ἔθνος: Greek word meaning "nation, peoples, or Gentile"
- Apostle: Greek word meaning "one who is sent"; those commissioned by Jesus to declare his will to the church and to be personal witnesses of him

Essay Questions

Short

1. Why is the Gentile centurion a model of faith? What does this teach us about God's redemption?

2. What three suggestions does Bock give regarding "times of the Gentiles"? Do you agree with him?

3. Paul continued to minister to the Gentiles as well as the Jews without losing sight of his identity as a Jew. How can a believer maintain respect for their culture or background while remaining faithful to God's Word?

Long

1. How does Luke-Acts explore more deeply the theology of Psalm 2? What comfort can be given to believers even today from this Psalm? Does Psalm 2 teach an adoptionist view of Jesus's messianic status? Why or why not?

Quiz

1. A Greek word Luke used prominently in referring to the Gentiles is:
   a) λαός
   b) Ἰσραήλ
   c) Ἰουδαῖος
   d) ἔθνος

2. In his infancy, Jesus was held by _____, who prophesied that the salvation of God would extend to the Gentiles.

   a) Simeon
   b) Elizabeth
   c) Anna
   d) Zechariah

3. Luke's genealogy ends with:

   a) David
   b) Abraham
   c) Adam
   d) Joseph

4. Jesus's arrest was:

   a) Unplanned, but responded to by God
   b) A surprise to Jesus
   c) Decided beforehand by God
   d) None of the above

5. In contrast to how earthly rulers use their power, disciples are called to:

   a) Hide
   b) Serve
   c) Poverty
   d) Lordship

6. James defended the inclusion of the Gentiles into the church by appealing to the prophecy of David's tent being rebuilt in:

   a) Hosea 1
   b) 2 Samuel 7
   c) Isaiah 11
   d) Amos 9

7. Which of the following was NOT required of Gentile converts after the council of Jerusalem?

   a) Refraining from strangled food
   b) Accepting of circumcision

c) Refraining from eating blood
  d) Refraining from fornication

8. Jesus's task of being a light to the nations was continued by:

   a) His angels
   b) The fall of Israel
   c) His commissioned servants
   d) The Holy Spirit alone

9. Luke showed in Acts that God was calling the nations away from their:

   a) Idolatry
   b) Heritage
   c) Names
   d) Memory

10. Jews and Gentiles at times reacted with hostility to the gospel because:

    a) They did not want to leave their homelands.
    b) It was an encouragement to them to cease religious action.
    c) They were afraid of disrespecting their rulers.
    d) It was a threat to the way they had lived.

ANSWER KEY

1. D, 2. A, 3. C, 4. C, 5. B, 6. D, 7. B, 8. C, 9. A, 10. D

CHAPTER 14

The Church and the Way in Luke–Acts

You Should Know

- The source of the imagery in Luke's use of "The Way" initially conveyed or alluded to Isaiah and Malachi.

- Luke 1:76: "And you, child [John], will be called the prophet of the Most High; for you will go before the Lord to prepare his ways."

- Luke 7:28: "I tell you, among those born of women none is greater than John. Yet the one who is least in the kingdom of God is greater than he."

- Acts 7:59–60: "And as they were stoning Stephen, he called out, 'Lord Jesus, receive my spirit.' And falling to his knees he cried out with a loud voice, 'Lord, do not hold this sin against them.' And when he had said this, he fell asleep."

- When the early church began to be persecuted, they responded by praying to the Lord for boldness to be given to them.

- The first time the term ἐκκλησία is used in Acts is at the judgment of Ananias and Sapphira.

- In Acts, Luke commonly utilizes the word "the Way" to describe the movement as a whole.

- In Acts, Luke commonly utilizes the word "the church" to describe the local community.

- ἐκκλησία: the Greek word for "church" or "assembly"

- The Way: Luke's unique motif to describe the church and its movement

Essay Questions

Short

1. What is the theological significance of the Christian community being called "the Way"?

2. How did Luke employ the word "church" in the book of Acts?

3. How did "the Way" make a social impact on the city of Ephesus? Should we expect the gospel to make social impacts in our own day?

Long

1. What are the four key activities used to describe the work of the early church? Is this normative for the church today? Why or why not?

Quiz

1. The Greek word used for "church" is:
   a) ἐκκλησία
   b) ὁδός
   c) Χριστιανός
   d) θεοῦ

2. Luke used a unique motif to describe the church, calling the church:
   a) The Way
   b) The Gospel
   c) The Truth
   d) The Community

3. "The way" was initially an image from:
   a) Jeremiah and Ezekiel
   b) Hosea and Habakkuk
   c) Isaiah and Malachi
   d) Kings and Chronicles

4. The one who prepared the way for the Lord was:
   a) John the Baptist
   b) Simon Peter
   c) Paul
   d) Mary

5. Per Bock, Stephen's use of the term ἐκκλησία in Acts 7 was:
   a) Technical
   b) Generic
   c) Particular
   d) Adverbial

6. The first time the term ἐκκλησία was used occurred:
   a) At the ascension of Jesus into heaven
   b) In Stephen's speech before the leaders of Israel
   c) At the judgment of Ananias and Sapphira
   d) During the conversion of Paul

7. Paul was journeying to _____ when he was confronted by Jesus.
   a) Damascus
   b) Antioch
   c) Jerusalem
   d) Emmaus

8. Believers were first called "Christians" by:
   a) The apostles
   b) Their opponents
   c) Jesus Christ
   d) The Holy Spirit

9. In Acts, "the Way" commonly refers to:
   a) The local community
   b) The apostles
   c) The city
   d) The movement as a whole

10. In Acts, "the church" commonly refers to:
    a) The local community
    b) The apostles
    c) The city
    d) The movement as a whole

ANSWER KEY

1. A, 2. A, 3. C, 4. A, 5. B, 6. C, 7. A, 8. B, 9. D, 10. A

CHAPTER 15

Discipleship and Ethics in the New Community

You Should Know

- Jesus's teaching to his disciples on how the world will respond to them indicates it will persecute them.

- Luke 21:34–36: "But watch yourselves lest your hearts be weighed down with dissipation and drunkenness and cares of this life, and that day come upon you suddenly like a trap. For it will come upon all who dwell on the face of the whole earth. But stay awake at all times, praying that you may have strength to escape all these things that are going to take place, and to stand before the Son of Man."

- The failure of the disciples at Jesus's betrayal prove that they needed the Spirit of God.

- Jesus encouraged believers to live in light of the end of time on this side of heaven.

- Luke 24:45–49: "Then he opened their minds to understand the Scriptures, and said to them, 'Thus it is written, that the Christ should suffer and on the third day rise from the dead, and that repentance for the forgiveness of sins should be proclaimed in his name to all nations, beginning from Jerusalem. You are witnesses of these things. And behold, I am sending the promise of my Father upon you. But stay in the city until you are clothed with power from on high.'"

- μαθητής: the Greek word for "disciple"
- Disciple: one who is a pupil or learner under a teacher
- διδάσκαλος: the Greek word for "teacher"
- Interpretations of the parable of the sower: Those with a good heart hold fast to the word that bears fruit; the riches of life choke out the word; persecution causes some people to fall away; Satan takes away the word before it can be planted.

Essay Questions

Short

1. What are several of the ways Luke showed in his works that one ought to love God and neighbor? How can such examples be models for believers now?

2. Describe how Luke showed the importance of faith and dependence upon God. How can you counsel someone struggling to look away from themselves and to look at Christ instead?

3. What types of people are called into the kingdom of God according to Luke? How can we be encouraged in our evangelism by this?

Long

1. Briefly describe in your own words the five church functions Bock lists. Which of these functions do you think continue in the modern church and how can they be exercised?

Quiz

1. The Greek word for "disciple" is:
    a) λαός
    b) ἀπόστολος
    c) μαθητής
    d) ἀρξιερεύς

2. Disciple means: (p. 315)

   a) One sent
   b) Learner or pupil
   c) Believer
   d) Speaker or proclaimer

3. Jesus called himself the _____ of the Sabbath.

   a) Lord
   b) Servant
   c) Follower
   d) Opponent

4. Which of the following is not one of Jesus's interpretations of the parable of the sower?

   a) Those with a good heart hold fast to the word that bears fruit.
   b) The riches of life choke out the word in some hearers.
   c) Persecution causes some people to fall away.
   d) A wicked servant will hide the seed given to him or her.

5. The Greek word for "teacher" is:

   a) διδάσκαλε
   b) ἀπόστολος
   c) πατήρ
   d) ἱερεύς

6. Jesus taught his disciples that the world would:

   a) Follow them
   b) Ignore them
   c) Persecute them
   d) None of the above

7. The failure of the disciples at Jesus's betrayal proved that they needed:

   a) Courage
   b) More disciples
   c) To listen to him
   d) The Spirit of God

8. Jesus encouraged believers to live in light of:
   a) The leadership of the apostles
   b) The fall of Jerusalem
   c) The redemption of the Gentiles
   d) The end of time

9. The New Testament writer who wrote most about the use of wealth and money is:
   a) Matthew
   b) Luke
   c) Paul
   d) James

10. The first individuals to hear that Jesus was risen from the dead were:
   a) Women
   b) The apostles
   c) The Pharisees
   d) The Sadducees

ANSWER KEY

1. C, 2. B, 3. A, 4. D, 5. A, 6. C, 7. D, 8. D, 9. B, 10. A

CHAPTER 16

How Response to Jesus Divides: The Opponents, the Crowds, and Rome as Observer of Events in Luke–Acts

You Should Know

- Luke 4:14–15: "And Jesus returned in the power of the Spirit to Galilee, and a report about him went out through all the surrounding country. And he taught in their synagogues, being glorified by all."

- Acts 5:17–18: "But the high priest rose up, and all who were with him (that is, the party of the Sadducees), and filled with jealousy they arrested the apostles and put them in the public prison."

- The only time that a priest was used negatively in Luke's gospel was in the parable of the good Samaritan.

- Jesus claimed he had authority over sin and the Sabbath, causing outrage amongst the Pharisees.

- Luke 8:46–48: "But Jesus said, 'Someone touched me, for I perceive that power has gone out from me.' And when the woman saw that she was not hidden, she came trembling, and falling down before him declared in the presence of all the people why she had touched him, and how she had been immediately healed. And he said to her, 'Daughter, your faith has made you well; go in peace.'"

- Luke 18:35–39: "As he drew near to Jericho, a blind man was sitting by the roadside begging. And hearing a crowd going by, he inquired what this meant. They told him, 'Jesus of Nazareth is passing by.' And he cried out, 'Jesus, Son of David, have mercy on me!' And those who were in front rebuked him, telling him to be silent. But he cried out all the more, 'Son of David, have mercy on me!'"

- After Jesus's miracles and teachings, the crowd thought Jesus was a prophet.

- In most of the instances in Acts where crowds were gathered together, their response was opposition.

- ὄχλος: Greek word for "crowds"

- Providence: the often-unseen daily actions of God in enacting his purposes

Essay Questions

Short

1. Who were the ones in the crowds most sensitive to Jesus's work and importance? What does this teach us about the gospel?

2. What did the crucifixion of Christ reveal about the crowds' response to him? In our own daily ministry, what should we expect from our interactions with the world?

3. Jesus's coming generated a reaction. Describe what this reaction meant then in the cultural complexities. If Jesus came in today's culture, what type of reaction do you think would happen?

Long

1. What are the similarities and differences between the crowds of Acts and Luke? How was the response of the crowds to the apostles a fulfillment of the promises Jesus made? How can knowledge of these promises help believers in preparation for ministry?

Quiz

1. Which of the following were NOT observers of Jesus?
   a) The Jewish leadership
   b) The crowds
   c) Rome
   d) None of the above

2. The chief priests were mostly comprised of:
   a) Gentiles
   b) Pharisees
   c) Sadducees
   d) Herodians

3. The only time "priest" was used negatively in Luke's gospel was in reference to:
   a) Herod's bribing the priestly class to his cause
   b) The consecrated bread that David took that was for the priests
   c) Gabriel's visit to Zechariah
   d) The parable of the good Samaritan

4. The group Jesus most often encountered with opposition on his way to Jerusalem was the:
   a) Sadducees
   b) Pharisees
   c) Herodians
   d) Romans

5. Jesus publicly claimed authority over _____ and _____, much to the anger of the Pharisees.
   a) Rome, the Temple
   b) Sin, Sabbath
   c) The Pharisees, the Sadducees
   d) Life, death

6. The Greek word that Luke most often used for the crowds was:
   a) ὄχλος
   b) πλῆθος

c) νότος

d) γραμματεύς

7. The blind man crying out to Jesus is the only one in Luke's gospel who uses the title:

   a) Christ
   b) Son of Man
   c) Son of David
   d) Son of Mary

8. Despite Jesus's miracles and teachings, the crowd as a group thought of Jesus as:

   a) A magician
   b) The Christ
   c) The Son of David
   d) A prophet

9. In most of the instances in Acts where crowds were gathered, the crowds primarily exhibited:

   a) Opposition
   b) Rejoicing
   c) Ambivalence
   d) Interest

10. The slave girl in Philippi who brings attention to Paul and Silas was:

    a) A Christian
    b) Curious
    c) Possessed
    d) Drunk

ANSWER KEY

1. D, 2. C, 3. D, 4. B, 5. B, 6. A, 7. C, 8. D, 9. A, 10. C

CHAPTER 17

Women, the Poor, and the Social Dimensions in Luke–Acts

You Should Know

- It would be absurd for someone making up the account of Jesus's resurrection to have him first appear to women when he arose from the dead, because in general, women were not allowed to testify in a court of law.

- Luke 1:26–30: "In the sixth month the angel Gabriel was sent from God to a city of Galilee named Nazareth, to a virgin betrothed to a man whose name was Joseph, of the house of David. And the virgin's name was Mary. And he came to her and said, 'Greetings, O favored one, the Lord is with you!' But she was greatly troubled at the saying, and tried to discern what sort of greeting this might be. And the angel said to her, 'Do not be afraid, Mary, for you have found favor with God.'"

- Luke 7:11–15: "Soon afterward he went to a town called Nain, and his disciples and a great crowd went with him. As he drew near to the gate of the town, behold, a man who had died was being carried out, the only son of his mother, and she was a widow, and a considerable crowd from the town was with her. And when the Lord saw her, he had compassion on her and said to her, 'Do not weep.' Then he came up and touched the bier, and the bearers stood still. And he said, 'Young man, I say to you, arise.' And the dead man sat up and began to speak, and Jesus gave him to his mother."

- Luke 8:1–3: "Soon afterward he went on through cities and villages, proclaiming and bringing the good news of the kingdom of God. And the twelve were with him, and also some women who had been healed of evil spirits and infirmities: Mary, called Magdalene, from whom seven demons had gone out, and Joanna, the wife of Chuza, Herod's household manager, and Susanna, and many others, who provided for them out of their means."

- Luke 10:38–40: "Now as they went on their way, Jesus entered a village. And a woman named Martha welcomed him into her house. And she had a sister called Mary, who sat at the Lord's feet and listened to his teaching. But Martha was distracted with much serving. And she went up to him and said, 'Lord, do you not care that my sister has left me to serve alone? Tell her then to help me.'"

- When Jesus's mother was commended as blessed for having given birth to him, in response he taught obedience is more important than life.

- Luke 1:46–48: "And Mary said, 'My soul magnifies the Lord, and my spirit rejoices in God my Savior, for he has looked on the humble estate of his servant. For behold, from now on all generations will call me blessed.'"

- When Mary sings her *Magnificat*, she is looking to the future.

- Luke 6:20: "And he lifted up his eyes on his disciples, and said: 'Blessed are you who are poor, for yours is the kingdom of God.'"

- The danger that the parable of the rich man and Lazarus shows is ignoring the poor.

Essay Questions

Short

1. What does the woman who anoints Jesus's feet teach about the gospel? How can believers learn from this account in their own ministry?

2. Describe some of the examples of women ministering in the church in the book of Acts.

3. Explain Luke's theology of the reversal of the poor over the proud. What did it mean to Luke's original audience? How can this concept be applied to our culture today?

Long

1. What was significant about Jesus's first appearing to women when he rose from the dead? What are some of the examples that gave evidence to women's secondary status in Jewish society? How does Jesus's call to be last and serve others help in giving all believers a proper perspective on themselves and others?

Quiz

1. In Jewish law, women generally were:
    a) Allowed to testify in any legal case
    b) Allowed to testify in legal cases only when their male relatives were present
    c) Not allowed to testify in legal cases
    d) None of the above

2. Elizabeth was called _____ with respect to the law.
    a) Blameless
    b) A sinner
    c) Imperfect
    d) A prophetess

3. Jesus showed support for the widow of Nain by:
    a) Giving her money
    b) Healing her of her sickness
    c) Praising her for anointing his feet
    d) Raising her son from the dead

Women, the Poor, and the Social Dimensions in Luke–Acts

4. Mary Magdalene was once:

   a) Possessed
   b) A prostitute
   c) A Gentile
   d) Blind

5. Of the two sisters, Mary and Martha, which was sitting a Jesus's feet while the other worked?

   a) Both
   b) Martha
   c) Mary
   d) Neither

6. In Luke 11, Jesus taught the woman who praised his mother that:

   a) A mother is greater than the father.
   b) A father is greater than the mother.
   c) Life is more important than obedience.
   d) Obedience is more important than life.

7. One of the issues of the early church in Acts 6 involved:

   a) The translation of tongues
   b) The treatment of widows
   c) The necessity of baptism
   d) The acceptance of Jewish believers

8. When Mary sings her song, she is looking:

   a) At the present
   b) Back to the past
   c) Forward to the future
   d) None of the above

9. The parable of the rich man and Lazarus illustrated the danger of:

   a) Failing to invest
   b) Loving relatives
   c) Being rich
   d) Ignoring the poor

10. The following miracle never occurred in the Old Testament:
   a) Healing a leper
   b) Healing a blind person
   c) Raising the dead
   d) Transforming an object into something else

ANSWER KEY

1. C, 2. A, 3. D, 4. A, 5. C, 6. D, 7. B, 8. C, 9. D, 10. B

CHAPTER 18

The Law in Luke–Acts

You Should Know

- Per Bock, Luke saw "law-abiding" as applying to Jewish believers.
- Luke thought the law had no benefit in regards to salvation.
- John the Baptist pointed to the new era, but he belonged to the old era.
- In Luke's context, if the Pharisees loved the law like they claimed, they should embrace Jesus's kingdom message.
- Jesus proved the resurrection of the dead was found in the Torah by appealing to the burning bush incident.
- Stephen's overall argument in his speech before the Sanhedrin was that Israel had habitually resisted God.
- Peter's argument for the Gentiles being included in the church without circumcision was that they had the Holy Spirit.
- Paul circumcised Timothy because his mother was Jewish.
- James wanted Paul, upon his return to Jerusalem, to support the four Jewish men's vow because he wanted to disprove the claims that Paul was against Jewish customs.
- Paul taught that the meaning of the Prophets and Moses was that the Messiah would suffer and rise from the dead.

Essay Questions

Short

1. What are the main interpretive views on Luke's theology of the law?

2. Briefly describe the theological points Luke made concerning the Law of Moses.

3. What does Acts 15 teach about the relationship of the law to the Gentiles?

Long

1. Explain and summarize the five views that Bock discusses in exegeting Luke 16:17. Do you agree with his conclusion? Why or why not?

Quiz

1. According to Bock, Luke believed that "law-abiding" was only a consideration for:
   a) Gentile believers
   b) Jewish believers
   c) Roman believers
   d) None of the above

2. Luke saw the law as providing _____ for salvation.
   a) The only way
   b) A necessity
   c) Some benefit
   d) No benefit

3. In Luke's context, if the Pharisees loved the law like they claimed, they ought to:
   a) Become Sadducees
   b) Oppose Jesus's kingdom message
   c) Flee Jerusalem
   d) Embrace Jesus's kingdom message

4. Jesus proved the resurrection of the dead is found in the Torah by appealing to:
   a) The taking up of Enoch
   b) The burning bush incident
   c) Joseph's bones being carried out of Egypt
   d) The death of Korah

5. According to Jewish tradition, Pentecost was the day:
   a) The law was given to Moses
   b) The Holy Spirit would come
   c) The Messiah would come
   d) The Messiah would ascend

6. In Peter's speech in Acts 3, he said that Jesus was a prophet like:
   a) Elijah
   b) Isaiah
   c) Elisha
   d) Moses

7. Stephen's speech in Acts 7 argued that Israel:
   a) Was becoming Roman
   b) Always accepted the promises of God
   c) Had habitually resisted God
   d) Was a new entity

8. Peter argued that Gentiles are included in the new covenant without circumcision because:
   a) They have the Holy Spirit.
   b) They are baptized.
   c) They will become circumcised.
   d) They are part of the church rather than part of Israel.

9. In Acts 21, James asked Paul to support four Jewish men's vow because:
   a) He wanted to force Paul's hand to support the Judaiziers.
   b) He wanted to disprove the claims that Paul was against Jewish customs.
   c) The Romans were coming to end Jewish sacrifices.
   d) The Jews were searching for a man to teach them.

10. Paul taught that the meaning of the Prophets and Moses was:
    a) Righteousness could be attained by works.
    b) Moses was superior to all others in the Old Testament.
    c) The Messiah would suffer and rise from the dead.
    d) Gentiles were forbidden from having the covenant promises.

ANSWER KEY

1. B, 2. D, 3. D, 4. B, 5. A, 6. D, 7. C, 8. A, 9. B, 10. C

CHAPTER 19

Ecclesiology in Luke–Acts

You Should Know

- The relationship between the early church and the synagogue includes: the church was forced out by the synagogue; the church continued to engage with the synagogue; the church became an independent community distinct from the synagogue

- The church was forced to become distinct from their Jewish heritage because of the persecution from the Jews.

- Jesus rules his church from God's side in heaven.

- The apostles were qualified to exercise leadership over the church because they were appointed to be Jesus's witnesses.

- The earliest response of the Jews to the gospel before they began to have a mixed attitude was that they strongly accepted it.

- Jesus told the apostles to preach the gospel to all nations. They first believed he was commanding them to preach the gospel to Jews who are in every nation.

- Jesus wept when he saw Jerusalem because he knew God was going to "visit" in judgment.

- Jesus's appearance in heaven during Stephen's trial signified that he was vindicated.

- After his study of Luke–Acts, Bock thinks maturity is the key qualification for leadership roles.

- *Gezerah shewa*: a Hebrew hermeneutical method where texts or events are linked by the use of the same word

Essay Questions

Short

1. Why is the outpouring of the Spirit important to understanding the church? What does the Spirit-indwelt church teach about the difference between the church now and the church at the second coming of Christ?

2. If the Old Testament anticipated the inclusion of the Gentiles, why did the early church struggle so much with their inclusion? Why is God's direct intervention to include the Gentiles with Cornelius's household important to the movement of the early church?

3. What do Luke's accounts of Peter and James teach us about the gospel?

Long

1. Briefly describe how the church is tied to both the old and the new. How is this helpful for understanding the church today? In what ways did the church become distinct from Judaism of its day?

Quiz

1. The relationship between the early church and the synagogue includes the following:
    a) The church was forced out by the synagogue.
    b) The church continued to engage with the synagogue.
    c) The church became an independent community distinct from the synagogue.
    d) All of the above

2. The church was forced to become distinct from their Jewish heritage because of:
    a) Logistics
    b) Her worldwide reach
    c) Gentile persecution
    d) Jewish persecution

3. The Hebrew hermeneutical method of *gezerah shewa* is:

   a) Texts or events are linked by the use of identical syntax.
   b) Names are used to provide hidden meanings.
   c) Events are linked by similar dates.
   d) Texts or events are linked by the use of the same word.

4. Jesus rules his church:

   a) From God's side in heaven
   b) Only during his earthly ministry
   c) From a national throne in Israel
   d) None of the above

5. The apostles were qualified to exercise leadership over the church because they were appointed to be:

   a) Kings
   b) Priests
   c) Witnesses
   d) Prophets

6. At first, the apostles thought that when Jesus said to preach the gospel to all nations he was referring to:

   a) Gentiles who are in every nation
   b) The eastern nations
   c) Jews who are in every nation
   d) Just Jerusalem

7. Jesus wept when he saw Jerusalem because:

   a) God was going to "visit" in judgment.
   b) God was going to "visit" Rome instead of Jerusalem.
   c) God would forget about Israel.
   d) None of the above

8. The first time Luke used the term "sinner" was:

   a) After Peter's miraculous catch of fish
   b) When Zechariah did not believe the angel Gabriel
   c) At Judas's betrayal
   d) In Mary's song

9. Jesus's appearance in heaven during Stephen's trial showed:
   a) Stephen was an apostle.
   b) Peter should be at the trial.
   c) Stephen was sinning.
   d) Stephen was vindicated.

10. According to Bock, the key qualification for leadership roles is:
    a) Faith
    b) Maturity
    c) Knowledge
    d) Skill

ANSWER KEY

1. D, 2. D, 3. D, 4. A, 5. C, 6. C, 7. A, 8. A, 9. D, 10. B

CHAPTER 20

Eschatology, Judgment, and Hope for the Future in Luke–Acts

You Should Know

- The basic division of Luke's eschatology is promise and fulfillment.
- The "already" of Luke's eschatology is the church age of the indwelling Spirit.
- The "not yet" of Luke's eschatology is Christ's return to reign.
- Peter thought repentance is necessary in order to participate in God's program of redemption from start to finish.
- Jesus predicted the fall of Jerusalem as the first coming judgment.
- Jesus predicted the second coming of Christ as the second coming judgment.
- The eschatological significance of the ascension of Jesus was that it inaugurated the present age.
- Luke connected Adam's defeat to Jesus's victory over Satan in the wilderness.
- Luke and Acts teach that when a person dies, they go immediately to be with Jesus.
- ἐλπίς: the Greek word for "hope"

Essay Questions

Short

1. How does Jesus's own example of suffering and then exaltation relate to the church's life in the already/not yet? Is there any comfort in this for believers today? Why or why not?

2. How did Luke present duty as a motivation for faithfulness? Is there a place to counsel others by appealing to duty?

3. What was the theology of "hope" in the book of Acts? How is this helpful for the church today?

Long

1. Explain the tension between the imminence and the delay of Christ's return. Do we still experience this tension? How is Luke's already/not yet eschatology helpful in knowing how to live in this age? How can you counsel others with this knowledge?

Quiz

1. The basic division of Luke's eschatology is between:
    a) Promise and fulfillment
    b) Law and gospel
    c) Israel and the church
    d) Humiliation and exaltation

2. The "already" of Luke's eschatology is:
    a) The church age of the indwelling Spirit
    b) Jesus's earthly ministry
    c) Christ's return to reign
    d) The giving of the law

3. The "not yet" of Luke's eschatology is:
    a) The church age of the indwelling Spirit
    b) Jesus's earthly ministry
    c) Christ's return to reign
    d) The giving of the law

4. For Peter, _____ is necessary in order to participate in God's program of redemption from start to finish.

    a) Repentance
    b) Knowledge
    c) Baptism
    d) Judaism

5. Jesus predicted that the second judgment to come would be:

    a) The fall of Rome
    b) The fall of Jerusalem
    c) The ascension of Christ
    d) The second coming of Christ

6. Jesus's ascension:

    a) Inaugurated the present age
    b) Consummated the present age
    c) Raised the dead
    d) None of the above

7. Jesus's victory over Satan in the wilderness is connected in Luke's gospel to:

    a) Peter's catching of fish
    b) Herod's persecution of Jesus
    c) Adam's defeat
    d) The exodus

8. In the Olivet Discourse, Jesus predicted the destruction of:

    a) Rome in AD 410
    b) Rome in AD 455
    c) Jerusalem in AD 70
    d) Jerusalem in AD 67

9. Jesus discussed much of his eschatological theology at:

    a) The Sermon on the Plain
    b) The Olivet Discourse
    c) The Sermon on the Mount
    d) The baptism of John

10. Luke and Acts teach that when a person dies:
    a) They go immediately to be with Jesus.
    b) Their soul goes into suspended animation or soul sleep.
    c) They are given their resurrected bodies to await the coming of Christ.
    d) They go to purgatory.

ANSWER KEY

1. A, 2. A, 3. C, 4. A, 5. D, 6. A, 7. C, 8. C, 9. B, 10. A

CHAPTER 21

The Scriptures in Luke–Acts

You Should Know

- At the time of Acts, the world would have viewed new movements with skepticism.

- Paul could speak for Jesus because the Spirit of Christ speaks through him.

- For the Jews, before the coming of Christ, their era was the era of law and prophets. For the pagans, this was the era of ignorance.

- Acts 4:10–12: "Let it be known to all of you and to all the people of Israel that by the name of Jesus Christ of Nazareth, whom you crucified, whom God raised from the dead—by him this man is standing before you well. This Jesus is the stone that was rejected by you, the builders, which has become the cornerstone. And there is salvation in no one else, for there is no other name under heaven given among men by which we must be saved."

- The coming of the Spirit proved that Jesus is Lord and Christ.

- The Davidic covenant promise was that a descendant of David would sit on David's throne.

- In Acts 3, the primary covenant to which Peter tied the promises given to Israel was the Abrahamic covenant.

- The most likely reason that Jesus was seen "standing" when Stephen died rather than sitting was because Jesus welcomed and vindicated him.

- Jewish perception of the Gentiles was an early stumbling block to the full inclusion of Gentiles in the church. God forced its implementation using visions and radical conversion.
- Paul's method of evangelizing when he was preaching was to do so first to the Jew, then to the Gentile.

Essay Questions

Short

1. Explain and discuss the scriptural theme of promise and covenant as found in Luke-Acts. How does Luke weave this theme into his narrative?

2. Explain and discuss the theme of Christology as found in Luke-Acts. How does Luke weave this theme into his narrative?

3. Explain and discuss the theme of community mission, community guidance, and ethical direction. How does Luke weave this theme into his narrative?

Long

1. Explain and describe Bock's first, second, and third axioms for Luke's interpretation of Scripture.

Quiz

1. At the time of Acts, the world viewed _____ with skepticism.
    a) Old movements
    b) New movements
    c) Polytheism
    d) Religion

2. Paul could speak for Jesus because:
    a) The Spirit of Christ spoke through him.
    b) He knew Jesus's words from the other apostles.
    c) Luke recorded the words of Jesus for him.
    d) He was a religious Pharisee.

3. What was an era of law and prophets for the Jews, was for pagans an era of:

   a) Infancy
   b) Knowledge
   c) Ignorance
   d) Law

4. The coming of the Spirit proved that:

   a) Peter was the head of the church.
   b) The Gentiles were judged.
   c) The Jews were judged.
   d) Jesus is Lord and Christ.

5. The Davidic covenant promised that:

   a) A descendant of David would sit on David's throne.
   b) Jesus would be called a Nazarene.
   c) Jerusalem would be the church's capital.
   d) All of the above

6. In Acts 3, Peter tied the covenant promises given to Israel to the:

   a) Adamic covenant
   b) Noahic covenant
   c) Abrahamic covenant
   d) Levitical covenant

7. Per Bock, it is likely that Jesus was "standing" when Stephen died because:

   a) Jesus stands whenever the church is persecuted.
   b) Jesus was interested in what was happening.
   c) Jesus welcomed and vindicated Stephen.
   d) Jesus was preparing for his second coming.

8. Based on the Jewish perception of the Gentiles, God had to force the implementation of Gentile inclusion in the church by:

   a) Appointing Gentile apostles
   b) Using persecution to drive the Jewish church outward
   c) Allowing the Jewish believers to learn it over time
   d) Using visions and radical conversion

9. Paul evangelized with the method of preaching:
    a) To the Gentile first, then to the Jew
    b) To the Jew first, then to the Gentile
    c) To Gentiles only
    d) None of the above

10. Peter showed from Leviticus that it is possible for a Jew:
    a) To be cut off
    b) To become a Gentile
    c) To obey the law
    d) None of the above

ANSWER KEY

1. B, 2. A, 3. C, 4. D, 5. A, 6. C, 7. C, 8. D, 9. B, 10. A

CHAPTER 22

Luke–Acts in the Canon

You Should Know

- Irenaeus defended Luke's apostolic credentials by appealing to the "we" passages in Acts.

- Lucan authorship is assumed by early church and undisputed by the end of the second century.

- Acts 1:1–2: "In the first book, O Theophilus, I have dealt with all that Jesus began to do and teach, until the day when he was taken up, after he had given commands through the Holy Spirit to the apostles whom he had chosen."

- Of the four gospel writers, Luke is the only one to record the ascension of Jesus.

- According to Bock, the role of the Holy Spirit is a focal point of Luke's theology.

- The feeding of the five thousand miracle is not unique to Luke.

- If we did not have Luke's writings, particularly Acts, we would miss Paul's three missionary journeys.

- Luke 8:21: "But he answered them, 'My mother and my brothers are those who hear the word of God and do it.'"

- 2 Peter 3:9: "The Lord is not slow to fulfill his promise as some count slowness, but is patient toward you, not wishing that any should perish, but that all should reach repentance."

- When discussing whether the activity in Acts is normative, Bock suggests God can be asked to do powerful things. And yet, the timing and nature of God's response are in his hands.

Essay Questions

Short

1. What are some of the parallels between Luke-Acts and the synoptic gospels? How are these parallels helpful in our understanding of the gospel?

2. What are some of the parallels between Luke-Acts and Pauline theology? How are these parallels helpful in our understanding of the gospel?

3. What are some of the parallels between Luke-Acts and the Catholic Epistles? How are these parallels helpful in our understanding of the gospel?

Long

1. What are some of the unique contributions Luke provides to the Bible in Luke-Acts? How can these be used to enhance our understanding of the gospel?

Quiz

1. Irenaeus defended Luke's apostolic credentials by appealing to:
   a) Luke's heritage as a Gentile
   b) The "we" passages in Acts
   c) Luke's presence at the Jerusalem council
   d) Peter's friendship with Luke

2. Luke's authorship of Luke and Acts was well attested in the church by:
   a) The end of the second century
   b) The beginning of the first century
   c) The end of the first century
   d) AD 325

3. (T/F) Luke contributed the largest corpus of writing to the New Testament.

4. Luke was the only gospel writer to record:
    a) The resurrection of Jesus
    b) The ascension of Jesus
    c) The crucifixion of Jesus
    d) The birth of Jesus

5. According to Bock, a focal point of Luke is:
    a) The appearance of miracles
    b) The role of Mary
    c) The role of the Holy Spirit
    d) The rejection of Jesus

6. Which miracle is NOT unique to Luke?
    a) The miraculous catch of fish at the call of Peter
    b) The feeding of the five thousand
    c) The Sabbath healing of a crippled woman
    d) The healing of the high priest's servant's ear

7. If we did not have Luke's writings, which of the following would we have no knowledge of?
    a) The resurrection of Christ
    b) The promise of the Holy Spirit
    c) Demas's betrayal
    d) Paul's three missionary journeys

8. (T/F) What Matthew and Mark present in a single discourse, Luke tends to distribute across his gospel.

9. (T/F) Luke viewed the delay in Christ's return as judgment, while Peter saw it as a delay that demonstrates God's patience.

10. Per Bock, God can be asked to do powerful things, but
    a) He will always answer positively.
    b) The timing of his response is contingent on prayer.
    c) The timing and nature of his response are in his hands.
    d) He will not answer.

ANSWER KEY

1. B, 2. A, 3. T, 4. B, 5. C, 6. B, 7. D, 8. T, 9. F, 10. C

CHAPTER 23

Conclusion

You Should Know

- Luke-Acts can be described as a "history of mission" narrative.

- The key actor in all of what Luke describes is God. It is his plan that is described.

- Six key theses about Luke's theology: Divine Direction, Salvation History, Continuity of Promise, and Mission; Israel's Story Includes the Nations and Is Not Anti-Semitic; The Spirit as the Sign of the New Era; Salvation and Identity Tied to Jesus' Work; A New Era and Structure in a Trinitarian Story; Realized Promise in Prophecy and Pattern

- Per Bock, Luke begins and ends his narrative with Israel.

- The program of God's salvation in Jesus Christ is different from that of other religions in that man cannot earn his salvation.

- Acts 5:30–32: "The God of our fathers raised Jesus, whom you killed by hanging him on a tree. God exalted him at his right hand as Leader and Savior, to give repentance to Israel and forgiveness of sins. And we are witnesses to these things, and so is the Holy Spirit, whom God has given to those who obey him."

- Luke's two volumes are about the mighty God who saves and who does so through Jesus Christ.

- The church's suffering can be seen best in light of an opportunity to faithfully witness to the fulfillment of God's promises.

- Luke's Gospel is the story of reassurance Theophilus needed to hear (Luke 1:4). But Luke's message and theology were not for Theophilus alone. The church still has the responsibility to carry this message to a world that needs such deliverance and reassurance.

Essay Questions

Short

1. How can Luke's theme of Israel's story including the nations without being anti-Semitic be used to help the church today in her mission?

2. How can Luke's theme of the Spirit being a sign of the new era be used to help the church today in her mission?

3. How can Luke's theme of realized promise in prophecy and pattern be used to help the church today in her mission?

Long

1. Explain and describe each of these six key theses about Luke's theology.

Quiz

1. (T/F) Luke-Acts presents the continuity of Israel's story with the new era that Jesus brought and the new community that his ministry generated.

2. Bock describes Luke-Acts as:
    a) Spirit-wrought biography
    b) History of mission
    c) Creative non-fiction
    d) The church's memoirs

3. According to Bock, Luke began and ended his narrative with:
    a) Israel
    b) Paul
    c) The apostles
    d) Mary

4. (T/F) Israel's story was about promise, which did not include the promise to include the nations in blessing.

5. According to Luke, the Spirit:
   a) Is a spirit of prophecy
   b) Purges humanity
   c) Enables mission
   d) All of the above

6. The program of God's salvation in Jesus Christ is different from that of other religions because:
   a) Man is the center
   b) Man can earn his salvation
   c) Man cannot earn his salvation
   d) None of the above

7. (T/F) According to Bock, Luke-Acts tells a Trinitarian story.

8. The new community of Christ is really what kind of faith?
   a) New
   b) Old
   c) Different
   d) Radical

9. The church's suffering is a/an:
   a) Response to forsaking the Jewish people
   b) Result of the inclusion of Gentiles
   c) Sign of God's judgment upon the church
   d) Opportunity to faithfully witness to the fulfillment of God's promises

10. Luke's story is the story of reassurance that who needs to hear?
    a) Theophilus
    b) Peter
    c) The world
    d) A & C

ANSWER KEY

1. T, 2. B, 3. A, 4. F, 5. D, 6. C, 7. T, 8. B, 9. D, 10. D

Notes

www.ingramcontent.com/pod-product-compliance
Lightning Source LLC
LaVergne TN
LVHW030634080426
835508LV00023B/3371